Scoliosis

My daughter has it.

A Mother's Story.

By

Annette Foster.

First published in 2018

MY DAUGHTER HAS SCOLIOSIS.

Chapter 1.

"Your daughter has scoliosis" the doctor said. I just stared back at him with the word scoliosis running through my head. What was it, how did she get it, but most of all, whatever it was my daughter had it!

Suddenly the doctor had started speaking to me again and woke me up from my thoughts, "it's a curve in her spine." He showed me that her spine in her back had started off in the right place at the top of her neck then swung to the right and then back straight again making an "S" shape. "Don't worry?" he said, "it can be sorted the hospital will be in touch." We left the doctors surgery in a bit of a blur, we felt shocked at what we've just been told.

There were so many questions I needed answering, most of all, what caused it? At the age of thirteen was it a too heavy rucksack filled with college books, was it sitting at the wrong angle. Why had I not noticed it earlier, this was October 2010 she had been swimming all summer in a swimsuit why had I not noticed it then.

Then one evening she had an itchy back and had asked me with my long nails to scratch it for her, that's when I noticed it. Her right shoulder blade looked dropped and was poking out more than it should of, something certainly did not look normal. If she stood up straight her shoulders did not look level, these are things to look out for should you find yourself in my position. Often, I've been told that hairdressers spot it, as when the child sits in the chair their back does not sit flush to the seat.

Chapter 2.

Our first visit to the hospital to meet the surgeon, we felt scared and nervous with so many questions that needed answering and how was life as we knew it going to change. An x-ray was done first, my daughter was given a gown to wear and the top half of her body was x-rayed. I went into the x-ray room with her, this I'm afraid was the first of so many more x-rays and visits to the hospital. We finally met our surgeon, he showed us the x-ray, I think all the talk cannot prepare you for what you are about to see for the first time, we have seen so many x-ray pictures since that they are second nature to us now but the first one is the most upsetting. To see your daughter's spine curved so much you cannot believe that the body can still function normally with her spine so out of place. As a mother, you only wish it was you and not your offspring sitting beside you.

The surgeon told us that a back brace could be fitted if her curve was less than 45 degrees but that was out of the question for my daughter her curve was coming up as 47 degrees. Again, you question yourself, why did I not notice such a curve in her spine, such a lump on her back where her back-rib cage was poking out.

The questions that were answered gave us no peace of mind, there was no reason this has happened, it was just one of the things that happen to so many children and adults each year, it was not my fault that I did not notice it, it was not my daughters fault for carrying a too heavy rucksack. The medical world thinks it's probably genetic, but no-one knows for sure yet.

My daughter was x-rayed every few months for the next year, each time the curvature was progressing, the hospital and the x-ray department was now a familiar place. By now her rib cage was noticeable on her back, she was suffering from backache, her shoulders were unlevel and she was walking slightly lopsided. She was not as tall as she should be.

Chapter 3

In June 2011, a lung function test was done, the results came back reassuring with an FEV1 of 94% and an FVC of 90% predicted and examination was remarkable. She was at low risk of requiring post-operative ventilation. This all meant that her lungs were in no danger of being squashed!

An MRI scan was booked where her body was scanned, I was allowed into the room and touched her ankles, so she knew I was there for her. Her spinal cord was monitored so the surgeons knew where they were operating. They were thorough. It gave me great comfort to know that the team were specified in their field. They were good, very good.

Each visit back and forth to the hospital, each X-ray showed her curve progressing, the degree getting higher, until it had reached 65 degrees.

It was in the January 2012, just over twelve months since she was first diagnosed that I received a phone call from the surgeon's secretary, my hands were shaking, I knew what the phone call was going to be. The operation was booked for March 2012. A letter confirming everything will be sent in the post, be in the hospital the night before as it will be the first operation of the day booked for 8.00am.

In February 2012, a spinal cord monitoring took place, this was to see where her spinal cord lay so they knew where they were cutting her back and moving her spine. It sounded so frightening. A clinical photograph was taken, more blood was taken, and a pre-operative assessment was done.

One week before the operation was due, the last lot of tests were done, suddenly they found a heart murmur. How can this be, she has never had heart problems. They ran the tests again if it was still a problem the operation would be cancelled. We were so close to having her spine sorted. The tests this time were ok, the consultant thought the murmur was to do with her spine being out of place, making all her organs work harder. Everything was good to go.

The tests seemed never-ending, prodding, poking, hurdles to cross, all of which my daughter did without question.

Chapter 4

Although we had been waiting for this day for what seemed like forever, finally it was here. A restless night followed by a day that took its toll. We prepared for our hospital trip that afternoon, with bags packed for us both as I was staying the entire time my daughter would be in the hospital as there was no way I was going to leave a fourteen-year-old to face the unknown alone. She had bought her own pillow with her, pink with flowers on it, just a little reminder of home. We made the car journey to the hospital in silence, trying not to think of what the next 24 hours were going to bring.

Arriving at the hospital my daughter was booked in and we were shown to our room. One hospital bed, one put-me-up bed. We both picked at the evening meal on offer, it seemed like the Last Supper, neither of us hungry but feeling we ought to have something, that evening lasted such a long time, when finally, we thought we both better try and get some sleep, we needed all the strength we could muster to face the following day.

Saturday 3rd March 2012

Here it was, the day of the unknown, the day that was going to sort out my daughters back problems, the day of no return!

The surgeons came in to tell us what was going to happen, one of them handed me a piece of paper, I had to sign it, giving my permission for the operation to go ahead, I had to sign to say I would let the surgery continue even if the monitors failed, as they had her back open they needed to be able to continue, basically I gave it the ok for them to operate blind-folded if it was necessary. With shaky hands, I signed the paper, I signed the disclaimer, to say if anything went wrong it was not their fault. The anaesthetist came in telling us his part of the operation, the nurses came in to take blood pressure and other tests they needed to make sure everything would go ahead as planned. It was like Piccadilly Circus for an hour and it was only 7. O'clock in the morning. When everyone had left, my daughter showered and put the hospital gown on, suddenly it all seemed real, this was really happening.

Five minutes to eight in the morning the porters came to wheel the bed containing my precious child on board to theatre. I walked alongside her, stepping fast to keep up with the trolley pushers, the words "don't cry, don't cry" running through my head, fighting back the tears, the doors to the anaesthetist's room swung open and the clang of us stepped inside. The next few minutes were a blur, I nodded not knowing what I was nodding to, the calmness from the anaesthetist was reassuring, he had probably seen frighten children and bewildered parents so many times before, a needle went into my daughter's arm. The anaesthetist told her a joke and she laughed. I was told to kiss her which I did as instructed and whispered, "I love you, see you soon" and then she was gone, her eyes shut, under the anaesthetic. They wheeled her into the theatre room as I watched the doors close my world suddenly fell apart, I was no longer in control of the situation, my daughters fate was completely in someone else's hands, my knees buckled, and I collapsed in a heap and started sobbing.

Every thought went through my mind, what happens if it goes wrong, what happens if that was the last I saw of my daughter, what happens if she comes out paralyzed. The nurses told me to get out the hospital for an hour or so, get some fresh air, go for a coffee, Brandy was what I needed but a coffee was what I ordered, I needed to be calm and strong for when she came around.

I cannot remember how I spent or got through the next six hours, I went outside the hospital, walked into town, looked around the shops and walked back, I think I ate something but what I'm not sure, I went back to our room and waited, and waited the longest six hours ever. The television was on, but I wasn't watching, when all of a sudden, the door opened and there stood one of the nurses, calmly she said, it was over, the job done, all went well, and she would be back in a short while to collect me to take me to the recovery room. Oh my God, it was all ok, tears were welling up in my eyes, it was over, or that is was I thought back then, little did I know that years later it was still on-going, still having x-rays.

While waiting to be collected I started to shake through nerves unsure of what state my daughter was going to be in. I heard my name, the nurse was calling me to follow her, which I did like a dog following his master, walking one step behind till we reach the recovery room. There she lay, the room was quiet, nurses and the surgeon were busying themselves from the operation, there my daughter lay, her eyes were shut, she was wired up to monitors which kept bleeping, looking so fragile, looking bruised, looking tired. I touched her hand, waiting for her eyes to open there was no response, I looked at the nurse for an explanation, she smiled and softly said your daughter has still a lot of anaesthetic in her she'll wake up when she's ready, holding her frail limp hand looking at her face willing her eyes to open, I got my wish, they flickered open. "mummy's here" I whispered, "mummy's here." She nodded and uttered "am I on my own pillow?" smiling to myself I answered "yes" and her eyes fell shut again.

They wheeled the bed with my daughter still lying there motionless back to the sideward and wired her up again to every machine that was beside her, she was on a morphine drip for pain relief, she was on a glucose drip for liquid, she had a catheter fitted for toilet requirements, heart monitors to measure her heart rate, she was on fifteen minutes obs, so for the next few hours every fifteen minutes a nurse came in to take temperature, blood pressure and other routine observers to record on her chart.

Every so often she would open her eyes, wince in pain, teardrops in her eyes and say a few words then her eyes would shut and once again fell into a sleep, this carried on till tea time, the nurses had changed shift, a different one came in and told me I should eat something, I did as I was told, after all my daughter was going nowhere! On my return from the dining area, my daughter was crying, "where were you" guilt took over me, the minute my daughter had woken I was not there, tears rolling down my cheeks, "I am here now, how are you feeling?" "everything hurts so much" she replied. One thing you learn as a mother is that you hate seeing your children in pain, you would rather be hurting yourself, you would do anything take their pain away. The nurse upped her morphine. She was allowed some sips of water, then within a few minutes she bought the water back up, violently sick, the anaesthetic was not agreeing with her, this carried on for the next 24 hours, every time she had something to drink she saw it in a sick bowl a few minutes later. Life can be so cruel sometimes just when all you want to do is get better something is there holding you back, looking back on it now it was only a week out of our lives but while you'll going through it, it's like time stood still, my daughter was on the mend after such a lengthy and complex surgery to her spine yet the anaesthetic was making her feel worse, the stuff she was bringing up was the vile, her stomach now in pain through reaching so much. Those first 24 hours were heartbreaking to watch, they were tearful, emotional and I kept thinking we were never going to leave this hospital.

All through that first night just as I was drifting off to sleep, which I so was desperate for, every fifteen minutes a nurse would come in do her checks, wrote it down and then leave, sometimes without saying a word in case she woke you, but every time I heard the door click open I was awake.

After one of the worse night's sleep ever, I showered, had some breakfast, and felt ready to face what the day had in store. My daughter finally stopped being sick and started to eat something light, progress I thought, when you're in hospital it's the small things that suddenly become a big deal. Like keeping your meal down! And learning to walk again.

During the operation, the surgeons opened my daughters back from her neck down to just above her bottom, the full length of her back. They inserted two metal titanium rods the length of her spine, placed one each side of her spine and fixed all three together with nuts and bolts. It was fused with bone chips, this was done so when finally healed, skin graph would cover over the metal rods. They had to be very careful when placing the rods in as they were so near the spinal cord, one false move and she could have been paralysed. This straightened the spine to 15- degree curve far better than the 65-degree curve she had just before the operation.

The hospital we were in was a private hospital, but the surgeon did the operation under the NHS as our nearest hospital was full and my daughters operation was needed to be done sooner rather than later. In this hospital, my daughter was the twenty-first person to have this scoliosis operation. Although the surgeon had done those operations for twenty years. In the room next door was a young lady slightly older than my daughter who had the same operation the day before, it was good to see her progress she said to me that when she felt she was able to walk she would come and see my daughter.

After another sleepless night, we were now in day two, feeling groggy (that was for both of us) and hoping maybe today she would feel a little better, we woke and started another day. The anaesthetic was wearing off and the pain was kicking in. She was at an all-time low, laying there crying, feeling sick, being sick, she refused to eat anything in case of seeing it again, blood tests were done at regular intervals, blood pressure and temperature was also being taken regularly, morphine was upped again as the pain increased and a few tubes she was attached to were taken away, a good sign. She was made to roll from side to side to start movement, but it hurt, she said she felt like she was splitting into two.

I ate small snatches of food here and there. My parents arrived with food which I was grateful for, they watched her while I went to eat and got a coffee, I dare not leave her anymore for long, she was in enough stress. It was upsetting for them too, to see their grand-daughter in so much pain.

After a very long day we were both shattered and fell asleep, still being monitored during the night but not so often I managed to get a few much-needed hours of sleep then about 3.0am I heard a bang instantly I was awake only to see my daughter in her sleep had dropped the morphine button onto the floor, this had alerted the nurses who come rushing in, sorted it out and did their regular checks and left. Tired I fell instantly back to sleep. All too soon the morning nurses had arrived doing their change over checks and we were about to start on day three.

Once again, the day started off in tears, she tossed from side to side unable to find a comfortable place. The nurses came to wash her with a bed bath as she was unable to walk to the bathroom, they changed her sheets, a clever act of doing it while the patient still lay in the bed. She had a visitor, the girl from the room next door, with nurses either side of her, she walked gingerly into the room, they sat her down in the armchair next to the bed and left the girls to chat. She was at this point an inspiration for us, to see there was light at the end of a very dark tunnel. To prove that everything will be all right. She stayed for about an hour and the nurses came back to help her back to her room leaving my daughter with a little more determination than before.

After lunch things really started moving, a physiotherapist came in and made my daughter sit up for the first time in three days, it hurt, her face told me that, tears were welling. She had to sit on the edge of the bed, which took every ounce of courage she had. When you have an operation, you don't think of the recovery, that you may have to learn everyday things you took for granted before the operation. She lay back down and had finally some colour in her cheeks, progress was made, even if it was just sitting on the edge of the bed. By tea-time she said she wanted to eat something, her glucose drip had been removed so it was no longer feeding her. She had a small amount of food, but it did not matter, she had kept it down. Grapes was the fruit she picked at constantly, they were small, moist, and not a lot of energy involved. We had, at last, a good day.

During the night, the nurses did not disturb us until 4.00am for the checks of blood pressure, temperature, painkillers and emptying the catheter bag, these obs took about half an hour. Just as we had fallen back to sleep, 7.30am the changeover nurse came in for an update. Sleep was lacking greatly now, I think your body goes into auto-drive and adrenaline, you are surviving on such little sleep.

As we reach day four, I started to think how much longer we were going to be in here, all I wanted was to go home, to sleep in my own bed, I'm sure her recovery would be faster in her own surroundings.

She managed some breakfast, her appetite had returned, not fully, we were hardly eating steak and chips but enough. She looked brighter in herself, the morphine drip came off today, so she had a bit more movement, freeing her hand. Her hand where all the drips had been looked fragile and busied, the pain was still unbearable, and the tears once more rolled down her cheeks. The physio came in again and made her sit on the edge of the bed then made her stand up, nurses either side of her for support she stood, tears were now rolling down my cheeks, she screwed her eyes shut with the pain that was ripping down her back, at that moment the girl from the room next door had walked in unaided and said "hi." My daughter was in no fit state to answer with her eyes fixed shut I don't think she even knew she was in the room. The girl left, it was good to see her walking knowing this will be the next step my daughter will reach. The evening past uneventful and into a better night's sleep, we were not disturbed until 6.00am which was like heaven. I think you can cope with anything in the day if you have had a good night asleep.

We were now on day five, it felt like my whole world was in this hospital, life on the outside had stood still, I couldn't remember what the day or date was. My daughter had visitors every day, family, school friends, the girl from the room next door which gave me chance to leave the room, have a walkabout but I never left the hospital. I hadn't felt fresh air in days, no idea what the temperature was outside, I knew inside it was warm.

The day started with my daughter having some breakfast, a good sign, the nurses a short time after came and removed her catheter, another item at last removed from her. With my help, she walked very slowly to the bathroom, took one look at her messy hair, and moaned at the state of it, my daughter was back! Although she was walking aided by myself, you could see by her face that every step hurt. Every step was an effort, something she had been doing since the age of eighteen months she was suddenly having to learn again. And it was hard.

For all her meals that day she was made to sit in the chair beside the bed, to give her body movement, so bed sores didn't form, the road to recovery. By tea-time we had made a lot of progress, just by walking to the bathroom, the light at the end of the tunnel was in sight. That night was one of the best night's sleep we both had.

Thursday morning arrived, and my daughter finally could have a shower. I had to be in the bathroom with her, so sitting on the toilet seat I just stared at her back as she had to face the shower. I could see the dried blood, I could see the swelling, the bruises, the stitches, running the full length of her spine. I helped her to dry and get some normal clothes on instead of hospital ware. After breakfast, she was collected by one of the porters who took her for her first x-ray after the operation. I followed behind. The x-ray showed her spine was now curving at about 15 degrees. Her rods were made of titanium, a light nonmagnetic metal, it would not bleep going through the airport, but it would not bend completely like your spine would, for example, she would not be able to do a forward roll, just as well she was not a gymnastic. She would not be able to do a bungee jump, thank god! She could not do anything that involved g-force. Like some rides at theme parks.

By Thursday afternoon we said goodbye to the girl next door, it was her time to be discharged. It was a sad moment, we had only all met at the beginning of the week, but she was the one person that was constant in our lives all week. And seeing her progress every day we knew what to expect my daughter's progress was going to be the following day. The physiotherapist came and took my daughter for a walk along the corridor she had to manage going up and down some steps before she was allowed home. She did them wincing in pain and not saying a word but did them.

We were left alone most of the evening, seeing little of the nurses, only very occasionally coming in to do blood pressure and temperature checks. How a week can alter so fast, at the beginning of the week my daughter had major surgery, couldn't walk and was as sick as they come. Now hopefully tomorrow will be back in our own home.

Friday morning finally arrived, it felt like we had been engulfed in this room forever. After breakfast the nurses came and did the final checks, I rang my parents to come and get us. The surgeon came to discuss the x-ray taken yesterday, it was looking good, her curve spine was measuring 15 degrees. They talked about what to expect over the coming weeks. The discharge papers were signed, follow up appointments were booked. My parents arrived and after lunch, a sad farewell to the team that had seen us through that week, then we were in the car going home. My daughter was in the back seat surrounded by pillows to make the journey as comfortable as possible, including her pink pillow that had barely left her side.

Chapter 5

While my daughter had been in hospital I had arranged for a new bed to arrive, with a firmer mattress. This was so she could sleep better and give her more support after the operation. Arriving home, she saw her new bed and burst into tears, emotion had taken hold, we had not had a normal life for a week and so much had happened.

I had to redress the wound every few days to keep it clean, it looked horrendous. That first week at home, we hardly left the house, painkillers and antibiotics were taken at intervals throughout the day, making her sleepy. She dozed on and off all day, every day. She had to do some amount of exercises, so her body did not seize up, by the end of the week I needed to do some food shopping, she asked to come to get out the house, gladly I took her, some fresh air I thought would do her some good. Something normal. She wandered around the supermarket holding on to the trolley for support. By the time we got home, she was worn out, but it had done her good.

As the weeks past, she got stronger in herself, her eating habits returned, and her friends from school visited. Regularly exercising. Six weeks had now past, and her first hospital visit and physiotherapy session. Her x-ray showed a lovely nearly straight curve in her spine, it was fusing nicely. Her physio session was in a pool of warm water, floating about doing some light swimming. It was only half an hour and it wore her out. We had several more of these sessions, each one my daughter could do a little more, feeling less tired.

She returned to school after about twelve weeks, doing just mornings, leaving the lessons a few minutes before everyone else so she would reach her next class without being shoved about in the rush. I collected her lunchtimes, not quite ready for the school bus. Her attendance for the year was low, as to be expected. The end of term in July soon arrived which gave her the whole summer to continue to recover and hopefully start back in September in year 10 fulltime.

By the end of the summer, all her dressings were off and the scar that runs the full length of her spine was looking good, it was healing well. She amazed me by wearing tops that you could see her scar, she said to me that if she couldn't see it she forgets it's there. She was ready to tackle year 10 at school, the start of her GCSE's. She still was not allowed to do sport for fear of being knocked about or falling over, although it all looked good from the outside, things were still healing on the inside. There was part of her spine that when you ran your finger down the scar, a lower part had gone numb, years later she still has no sensation on that part of her back.

Life carried on normally, my daughter went back to school, did her GCSEs and the next few years flew by. Even at her school prom, she wore a beautiful ball gown, low at the back revealing at least half her scar.

Her scar was now fading fast. Her pain from the operation now just a distant memory.

Chapter 6

We were now in early 2014, my daughter was fine, I, however, was not. I had terrible back pain, then a trapped nerve was to follow. Pain was shooting down my leg with every step. Painkillers were not touching the sides of the pain which seemed to be getting worse. A trip to the doctors who prescribed strong painkillers and said I had sciatica. The trapped nerve was not shifting. I hobbled back to the doctors a month later still in severe pain. He booked a scan to see why the pain was not easing.

By Easter, I went for my scan and a trip back to the doctors for the results.

He peered over his glasses and said, "are you aware you have scoliosis." "No, I wasn't!" was my reply. "My daughter has it." He continued "It's heredity so I'm not surprised. Don't worry yours is not a bad as your daughter's. You have a slight curve 6 inches from the base of your spine. Not enough to notice but what has happened is that the nobbles on your spine has shifted slightly and are swollen causing a nerve to be trapped." I was prescribed the strongest anti-inflammatory tablets. It was a long healing progress because of the severity of my condition it took nearly another six months before the pain had eased.

By now we were in October 2014 and our next health problem was just around the corner.

Chapter 7

Life has a way of turning everything upside down. My daughter had now left school and was attending sixth form college. A Caribbean cruise with her father (who I had divorced years ago,) was booked in the following January 2015. My daughter who was now about to turn seventeen in the next month was now complaining of a backache. A lump on her scar was oozing with pus, we kept checking it daily and of course, it was getting worse, the lump was getting larger and more pus was oozing. Finally, I took her to the family doctors who told us to go to A and E at hospital, surely, it was only a fatty tissue forming, why the emergency department? So off to hospital once more. We waited to be seen with what seemed like forever, doctors came, paediatricians, as she was still under eighteen, nurses again taking bloods, blood pressure, temperature and all the other checks.

Suddenly and unexpectedly a junior doctor said, "infection on her spine". What, how can it be, her scoliosis operation was two and a half years ago, everything was fine, everything was healed. I wanted my surgeon, I wanted a second opinion. I wanted this nightmare to go away.

After six hours in the A and E department, we went home. An appointment was booked in a few days' time to see our surgeon. Our appointment came, he looked concerned "I have never seen an infection so long after the operation" he said, "we'll put her on a course of antibiotics and see me again in two weeks".

Two weeks came and went, still the lump was getting bigger and pus still forming, another two weeks off college. And here we are back in the surgeon's office, he should have been signing us off after three years. They keep an eye on you for three years after a scoliosis operation to make sure everything is progressing in the right way, instead, he was talking about more surgery. A date was set for another operation. It was in the next few days. "Overnight bag is only needed. You won't be staying with us for long" the surgeon was saying.

The day arrived, nil by mouth, we waited for our turn for surgery, we were in the children's ward, as my daughter was nearly seventeen but still a minor. The other children in a waiting ward seem so fragile and looked poorly, they all went for surgery one by one. By lunchtime and extremely hungry, at last, her name was called. She gowned up, once again I signed the piece of paper to allow the operation to go ahead. Once again, I walked with her to theatre and once again I kissed her cheek as she went under the anaesthetic and once again I cried as she was wheeled through the doors for surgery.

The nurses, doctors, and the surgeon team were all so calm, how many mothers do they have to support as our children are wheeled through the doors of the unknown. They have seen it all before but for us, it can be so overwhelming.

The next five hours were unbearable, I wandered, I paced, I tried to eat, I made phone calls. I could not believe I was, here again, doing major surgery, again. This time the surgeon was going to open her back along the original scar, flush special liquid around her spine and rods to wash the infection away. He would also take a biopsy to find out what caused the infection so long after the first surgery. I had faith in my surgeon, he knew what he was doing and that was all that mattered.

My phone buzzed, I answered it with shaky hands, "we're ready for you now, she's in the recovery room" said such a kind voice on the other end of the phone. I had a moment when I lost my bearings, how to get back to the recovery room, I wandered for a few minutes, eagerly looking for the signs on the wall telling me what direction to go in. Found it, hurried along the echoing corridor till I reach the door that said, "Please ring the bell," I rang and waited. I heard footsteps the other side of the door, the door swung open, I was greeted with "everything went well, she's this way." Following behind, there my daughter lay, looking weak and pale. Hooked up to all the machines, measuring heart rate, blood pressure oxygen levels. Machine bleeping. She opened her eyes, looked at me said she felt sick, I called the nurse, who came with a bowl, too late, all down the nurse's uniform. How embarrassing,

"I'm so sorry" I cried as I watched my daughter go from pale to green in colour as she threw up again. Here I was again holding her hair back as she had her head once more in a sick bowl.

Back to the ward several hours later the porters pushed her bed back through the long hospital corridors till we reach the bustle of the children's ward, not like the private side ward we had when the first operation was done, this had other people in it, this had crying upset fragile children in it, worried and tired looking parents in it. Nurses rushing about and monitors beeping. Her bed was tucked into the corner and I unloaded her bag for her overnight stay, thankfully she was not going to be here long. How naïve of me thinking it would be that simple. The overnight stay ended up being five days!

A Cannula in her small wrist had been inserted while she was under the anaesthetic where antibiotics were now being pumped and where painkillers were pushed into. Once again, her temperature was taken at regular intervals, bloods were taken to monitor her infection, had they got rid of it? Also, she had a cannula inserted on her upper arm, with a tube running inside her laying just under the skin reaching her main valve near her heart. This was so antibiotics could be pumped straight into her bloodstream and they could start taking effect immediately.

As this was only an overnight stay I decided not to take leave from work. I went home at the end of a very long day. After a restless night, I went to work the next morning. I left work at mid-day made the hour drive to the hospital in eagerness to bring her home. No such luck.

It was all too familiar. The anaesthetic once again did not agree with her and once again she was sick, very sick. She could not hold anything down, not even water. She was then given anti sick pills for her sickness. How many pills can one small delicate stomach take? She lay in her hospital bed looking pale, thin, and weak. It's heart-breaking as a mother to see your child laying like that and for a short while everything is out of your control.

My daughter's sickness started to subside, her appetite slowly came back, just picking at little pieces of food, but something was better than nothing. By day five she was once again well enough to go home, the cannula in her wrist was taken out but the one in her arm was to stay. That was how my week went, I went to work, left off at mid-day, drove to the hospital, stayed until the evening, went home to sleep, and repeated it the following day. There is only so much the body will take and I was feeling it by the time the nurses gave her the all clear to go home.

They set up a nurse to call at our home every day to administer drugs into her arm through the cannula, "how long for" I asked. "three months" was the reply. This was late October her cruise was early January.

So, that was our life on hold again, we were sent home and tried to live a normal life only our daily routine included a nurse calling every day to take blood pressure, take temperature and pump anti-biotics into my daughter's arm and every few days taking some blood samples to see what the level of infection was. In all of this she turned seventeen, some birthday!

Chapter 8

Two weeks later we went to see her surgeon for an update on how things were doing. My heart raced when he said, "the infection has not improved, it is getting worse instead of getting better, the operation we did has not worked." I was welling up, she has been through two major back operations and we are back to square one. "what's to be done now?" I managed to ask. "The rods need removing." "What" I almost yelled. "What do you mean the rods need to come out, we were told they are in for life." The surgeon removed his glasses from his face, looked at me then my daughter who sat there very quietly and explained, "the infection is clinging on the metal in her back, the only way we can now remove the infection is to remove the rods." I was struggling to understand, I knew this involved surgery again. "I have placed a lot of rods in for correction spine surgery, but I have removed very few, to have this much infection is very unusual especially after two and half years from when we put the rods in. The biopsy we took a few weeks ago is not giving us any answers on what is going on," he continued, "the only way to get rid of the infection is to remove the rods." "Is there no other way." I was trying desperately not to let her have another operation. "No" came the reply. This cannot really be happening, it was like a dream, a bad dream. "When do you want her back for surgery," I asked thinking we had time to get our heads around this situation. "Tomorrow, I want you back here for 11.00am." I sat there trying to take in what I was just told. "Tomorrow." "Yes. Tomorrow, this is a nasty infection she has, we cannot wait, it needs to be removed as soon as possible as it is working its way up her spine and making its way towards the brain" This now sounded serious, I didn't think till that point how serious this was.

We went home, packed for the following day, rang my parents. Notified her college that she was not coming back until the New Year. And asked my work for an emergency week off, I was not leaving her this time. We were now in mid-November. And early next morning set off for the hospital again. I knew every corridor of that hospital now, I knew all the wards that involved my daughter and some of the nurse's names when we arrived and booked in, we received greetings of "I remember you from a few weeks ago!" from some of the nurses.

Pre-med was given, I signed the papers giving consent for the surgery. Deja Vu, and we waited for her turn as we sat in the children's waiting ward. Everyone was so much younger than my seventeen-year-old. One by one they went off for their operation. Looking so brave, their parents feeling the same feeling that I was feeling. Then my daughter's name was called. My heart missed a beat, here we go again.

I followed the bed as it was wheeled along the long corridors into the theatre. The scared look on her face, the brave look on my face. The anaesthetist done his job made her count to ten, I kissed her cheek, I tried to whisper, "I love you" but it was some sort of mumble. By the time she had reached six in her counting, her eyes were shut, and she was under. I left the room with tears flowing down my cheeks. How could we be here a third time? How unlucky to have an infection so severe that another major operation was needed, the rods should have been for life, she should be enjoying a normal life, not back here having them removed.

This involved cutting her back open along the same scar that runs the full length of her back, chipping at the bone that had fused nicely holding her rods and spine in place. Unscrewing the nuts and bolts that were holding it all together, removing the titanium rods, putting the chipped bone back around the spine to hold it without the rods being there. The surgeon had told me that after two and a half years the spine should hold upright by its-self should the rods ever have to be removed.

I waited and waited for the next six hours, that seemed like a lifetime. I wandered down to the main complex of the hospital, waiting for my phone to vibrate. I ordered a coffee and sat at one of the tables. I watched people coming and going, wondering what had bought them to this place. People in wheelchairs being pushed by family or nurses, doctors on their lunch break, grabbing a sandwich and a hot drink. Young students queuing for a burger, probably on their lunch break from the nearest college, not poorly at all. The smell of freshly brewed coffee was twitching my nostrils, the hot smell of burger and chips making me suddenly feel hungry. Making me jump, lost in my thoughts my phone buzzed. Fumbling I answered it. "She's out of theatre." The nurse had said with such a calm voice. I made my way back to where I had left her, rang the bell, and waited for the door to open. A nurse opened the door and led me around the corner into the small recovery bay, and there she lay. Pale, and wired up to everything bleeping, monitoring her breathing, checking her heart rate, her weak frame laid in the bed, looking weary after major surgery. Then suddenly the surgeon appeared, "Everything went well, the rods have been removed, she did lose some blood and we performed a blood transfusion." At this point I was staring at him not sure if I heard him right. Loss of blood, blood transfusion. It hit me just how serious this operation had been.

The porter wheeled her bed back to the ward an hour later when they thought she was stable enough to be moved. I again trundled behind. Parked the bed in the bay and hooked her wires back up. I could not believe we were here again. I noticed we were in the same bay as two weeks previous. I knew what was coming next, the anaesthetic was going to make her sick, and as soon as she started to come around and the painkillers started to wear off, we were reaching for the sick bowl. The cannula was still her upper arm where they administer her painkillers and antibiotics, and an hour or so later the sick bowl was used. The next few days were the same, she couldn't eat. Sips of water were bought back up again, not until the anti-nausea drugs were given did the sickness start to subside. By the third day, things started to improve, all you want is to go home and all the nurses said was "not today." The nights were noisy everything always seems so much louder in the dark, other patients crying, being so much younger than my daughter, not aware of what was going on. Mothers trying to sooth them, nurses in and out of closed curtains giving painkillers and doing the night checks. The nights were long, and the days seemed even longer. My bed was a pull-down bed from a cupboard and a few blankets, during the day this was put back in its cupboard and a chair was placed for me to sit in all day. As she wasn't ill just being monitored, most of the time we were left alone.

My parents came and took me out of the hospital for something to eat, as I couldn't remember when I last eat properly. My daughter was under the care of the nurses for an hour. She wasn't going anywhere, unlike last time, she was now a few years older and wiser and we've been here before several times.

After five days, my daughter felt almost back to herself, eating, drinking, still slightly weak and sore, but well enough to go home. All we were waiting for the surgeon to discharge her and a medi- nurse to be in place to continue to administer the antibiotics at home through the cannula in her arm. This took another twenty-four hours to sort out. So, on the sixth day around lunchtime, we were given the all clear to leave.

You think the world stops while you're in hospital because for you it does but when you step outside you realise that the world has carried on without you.

Chapter 9

We went home and tried to lead a normal life, it's hard when a nurse comes in every day to your home to give drugs, painkillers, check temperature, check blood pressure, write notes about her findings. We had a big box full of her injections, syringes, bandages for her wound and her notes. We were now towards the end of November. My daughters cruise looming nearer. The infection levels were carefully watched, the nurses took blood samples regularly. She had been through so much in hospital and it was still ongoing. We had to make a once a week trip to the hospital to the infectious unit for a complete thorough checkup, more bloods taken, to watch the infection levels, this all become the norm for a while. It was a wonder she had any blood left in her the amount they took out.

My daughter did not return to college as they soon broke up for the Christmas holidays. Hopefully, she would return after her cruise, feeling better. Christmas day came, and we went to my parents' house, the nurse even called there, we took our medical box with us so everything the nurse needed was in it.

We had an appointment with the surgeon at the end of December, a review, he told us that the infections levels were at last easing. He wrote a note for her to take with her explaining why she was taking a lot of drugs on board the ship. Her cannula was removed. It had been part of her for nearly three months. She was glad to see the back of it. Although it did leave a small hole in her arm from where it had been for so long.

Early January and time for her cruise, her dad came and collected her and off they went. When she returned two weeks later she looked so much healthier than she did before she went, the sun and relaxation had done her good. Another hospital trip was made and at last the surgeon told us the infection had gone. The biopsy they took had gone to four different hospitals to find out what the infection was or how was it caused, it all came back inconclusive. No ones to this day knows what it was or the cause of such a nasty infection. An x-ray was taken, the first since before the rods were removed, her curve was measuring 38 degrees, it was not the best result, it meant without the rods her spine was starting to move again.

Chapter 10

My daughter continued her progress and tried to lead a normal life, it was only when she bent forward did her rib cage on her back become very noticeable. She returned to college but with such low attendance her heart was no longer in it, so she left for good and started to work part-time for our local supermarket. A job which she enjoyed and increased her hours over the course of time. By March that year, her back started to ache, looking worse as the hump on her back was now severely noticeable so I requested another x-ray to check on things. One was made a few weeks later. Off to the hospital again, it just seems never-ending. The routine was the same, we knew it off by heart, book in at children's clinic, then off to x-ray, then back to children's clinic for the chat with the surgeon. We did all of this and waited for our turn to see the surgeon. Her name was called, and we followed the nurse to the surgeon's room. "Yes, it has moved slightly" he was saying, "I knew it" I thought, "it is now measuring 45 degrees." He continued "It is not at a dangerous level, pre-operative her scoliosis measured 65 degrees. We'll x-ray her again in six months and go from there." We left the hospital, when will this stop, when will she be free from continually having visits to the hospital. Another check up was made for October that year. All we could do was continue with life until the next appointment.

October's check-up came and went, spine was still at 45 degrees, no further action required. Be back in twelve months. She continued to work at the local supermarket. The following October came, we were now four and a half years since her first operation and two years since the removal of the implants. Another x-ray showed her spine still sitting at 45 degrees, no change.

The surgeon that had been our savour over the past five years had retired. The thoughts of a new surgeon put panic in me, our surgeon I had faith in, such trust, he had been with us on this traumatic journey, he had been part of our lives for such a long time and now our case was being passed over to someone else.

We arrived at the hospital for the umpteen time, did the same thing as usual, booked in at the children's clinic, even though my daughter was now a week away from turning 19. But because she has been under the surgeon's care since the age of 12 they continued to see her. Next, she was x-rayed, then back to the children's clinic to wait for her appointment with the new surgeon.

Her name was called, and we followed the nurse to his room. It was a familiar face, he had assisted with our surgeon with her very first operation to put the rods in nearly five years ago and assisted with the removal of them. He had taken over as our new surgeon dealing in my daughter's case.

The x-ray had shown no movement, in his report he wrote. A repeat x-ray today showed a residual scoliosis measuring 45 degrees, the curve has progressed from the initial x-ray after the implants were removed at 38 degrees but her pre-operative x-ray her scoliosis measured 65 degrees. This recent x-ray has not changed in the last twelve months. He discussed the options my daughter now had.

The surgeon spoke with a calm, soft voice, "we can x-ray one final time in another twelve months, then if it still hasn't moved, we will discharge her, finally." We sat there nodding, although this was what we both wanted so badly to be discharged from this, it was also scary, because all the time she was having yearly x-rays, it was a back-up to know that everything was all ok. Without this, it was going into unknown territory, what if it started moving again and we didn't know. Coming to hospital once a year however tedious, it felt safe, that we were being kept an eye on.

The surgeon continued "if your daughter is really unhappy about her appearance, then we could operate and put the rods back, this is not going to be an easy operation as everything is fused around her spine and has settled down, but it can be done." As her curve is very noticeable when she bends forward, her back-rib cage pokes out giving a hump effect. He continued with the options. "If we x-ray in a year time and her spine curve has moved from where we are today then we have no choice but to put them back." At 45 degrees or more, the curve can look very unsightly. It can cause a problem with body image and self-esteem. It can cause backache and pain. In rare cases, a significant curve of the spine of 50 degrees or more can sometimes increase pressure on the heart and lungs. Which is why an operation to straighten the spine is necessary.

We left the hospital again with another twelve months hold on her life. Again, not knowing if she was going to be discharged or end up having another operation.

Chapter 11

The new year arrived and my daughter who by now had enough of putting her life on hold decided to start applying for some travel jobs, something she has always wanted to do but with operations always at the end of the tunnel she put them aside to work at her local supermarket, it was the safe choice.

She had managed at college to do one year out of a two-year course in Travel and Tourism. Something she said she would finish but never got around to it.

Suddenly in March 2017, she had three interviews lined up. All in travel. All to work abroad. The first was a skype interview, working for Euro-camp. The interview went well, and they said they would contact her in a few days. Next was an interview which was in a hotel too far away. When my daughter rang to cancel and explained why a telephone call interview was arranged. The third was an interview at the end of the week in a hotel in London, an hour on the train, which was doable.

Euro-camp emailed a few days later confirming she had the job!

My daughter cancelled the London one, as before this interview was to be held, a date for departure for the confirmed job was booked.

She had a lot of forms to complete and in little more than a week later I waved her off at the airport.

I drove home from the airport, I had such mixed emotions, A sudden loss of my daughter even though it was temporary, she was in France for the summer. Also, a sense of pride that she was, at last, achieving her dream, despite everything she has gone through. All the downs in her life, she was now doing something positive.

Her scar on her back, her rib-hump when she bends forward. These were things on her body that she will probably always have.

Nothing was going to discourage her. Her next x-ray was booked for October. But for now, she was living in France, getting paid while working in the sun.

Chapter 12

Having scoliosis puts you in the elite club.

On average 4 in 1000 children have scoliosis. At the time when my daughter was diagnosed, she found that in her school of around 900 that 3 other girls also had the condition.

At the time of writing this book, a petition was formed to allow screening at school at the age of 14 to see if anyone has the condition. Once the curve hits around 50 degrees surgery is the only option. If found earlier enough a back-brace could be worn to try to straighten the spine.

You'll find some people have never heard of the word and some people know someone that has it. And there are the famous people that have it too.

Like sportsman Usain Bolt.

The actress Daryl Hannah.

A musician Yo-Yo Ma

Madonna's daughter Lourdes Leon

And The Royal Princess Eugenie.

These people have told the world they have this condition, and then carried on with their lives and have gone on to do great things, or to be great people.

Ordinary people also do not let it take over their lives, they get on with everyday living.

Chapter 13.

My daughter came home from working aboard six months later, a stronger and more confident person. She had also turned twenty. She had told her work colleagues about her curve, they saw it when she was wearing her swimwear or just in her summer clothes, it did not stop her wearing what she wanted.

Her next hospital trip was in December 2017. It was meant to be October but with her not in the country, the appointment was rearranged. This could be her last trip, with any luck the surgeon will sign her off.

The day before her appointment she posted on her Facebook page photos of her x-rays, one before the rods went in, one with the rods in, and one with the rods removed, and a quote, it read; I have scoliosis, it is a condition that I live with, but it will not define who I am. This is me.

She had decided no longer to hide her scar that runs the full length of her back, no longer wanting to hide her back-rib-hump that sticks out like a dolphin fin every time she bends forward.

Chapter 14.

The day came, just as it always had, and once again for the um-teen time, we set off making the hour-long journey to the hospital.

On arrival we were sent to the x-ray department for what could be her final x-ray, this was so routine for us. With the x-ray done we headed off to the clinic.

It was a little different this time, we were no longer going to clinic 6, children's clinic. The new surgeon had decided that now my daughter had reached twenty, she should be seen in his adult out-patients clinic. It took us a while to find this new place, we could find clinic 6 blind-folded, but the new area proved a little harder to find.

When we finally arrived, we checked in and waited for her name to be called. We sat there chatting about all the times we had been at the hospital. Unfortunately, none of them happy memories. As her mother, I had been there, through all the lows and lower than low times. All the worries, all the sleepless nights, all the holding her hair out the sick bowl times. All the times wishing it was me and not my daughter.

Her name was called, off we followed the nurse to the surgeon's room. He done the normal formalities, shook hands, asked how she had been, any concerns, any pain. On the computer showed her x-rays, five of them. 2010 her first x-ray, showing a 65-degree curve. The second x-ray in 2012 showed a 15-degree curve with titanium rods holding her spine. In 2014, the third showed after the rods had been removed, a 38-degree curve, the fourth showing a 45-degree curve which was taken in 2016. And the fifth and final one in 2017 showed a curve at 47 degrees.

He talked about the showings on the screen. On how her curve had increased slightly but not enough to do anything about. In his opinion, he thought the spine had now found it's resting place and was unlikely to move any further.

He commented at my daughter's removal of her rods, he said he had been performing spine/ scoliosis corrections for more than ten years and in that time only ever removed rods three times, one being on my daughter.

He then said he would inform my daughter's doctor at our local surgery that she has been discharged from the hospital.

We shook his hands and left.

Chapter 15.

It was over. Nearly eight long years of hospital trips, three operations, lots of tears and unknowing as well as sleepless nights and worry.

My daughter suddenly felt vulnerable. With no more x-rays, she'll not know if her spine is still moving. She felt safe having these check-ups once a year. The surgeon telling her that everything was all fine. It was comforting, reassuring.

I feel like she has gone through so much and came through the other side. Lengthy operations, a scar that will not fade and a back-rib-hump that will be there forever more. Learning to walk again, being and feeling as sick as you can be.

My daughter is in work and happy with her body just the way it is, she has accepted that she must live with it and deal with it.

I am so very proud of my daughter and the young woman she has become.

As she said, it's who she is. This is me.

Scoliosis, my daughter has it. This is her mother's story.

These are the x-rays of my daughter's spine.

Until you see how far your spine can move, scoliosis is just a word.

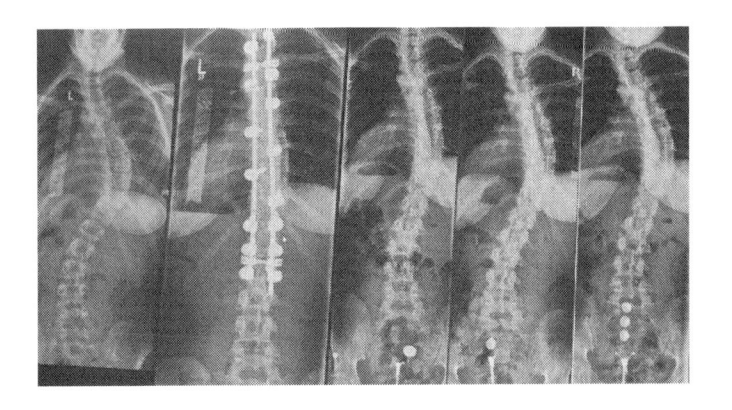

The first x-ray shows her spine before all the operations.

The second shows after the first operation with the rods holding her spine in place.

The third show after the rods were removed and the spine starting to curve once more.

The fourth and fifth show the final x-rays showing how her spine is now and where it will probably stay.

Thank you.

To the surgeons, doctors, nurses and all the hospital staff that cared for my daughter making her stays in hospital more bearable.

And thank you to our family and friends for all your love and support through some tough times.

For more information and help visit;

Sauk, - Scoliosis Association UK

A website that has all the guidance, reassurance and help that you need when dealing with a condition you know nothing about and knowing you are not alone.

Or you can always contact me, via my web site;
www.nettysnotebook.co.uk

Made in the USA
Columbia, SC
17 July 2018